LUX PERPETUA

Peace and unity

for SATB choir and orchestra

JONATHAN WILLCOCKS

MUSIC DEPARTMENT

OXFORD

UNIVERSITY PRESS

OXFORD
UNIVERSITY PRESS

Great Clarendon Street, Oxford OX2 6DP, England
198 Madison Avenue, New York, NY10016, USA

Oxford University Press is a department of the University of Oxford.
It furthers the University's aim of excellence in research, scholarship,
and education by publishing worldwide

Oxford is a registered trade mark of Oxford University Press
in the UK and in certain other countries

7 9 10 8 6

ISBN 978-0-19-338742-3

Printed in Great Britain on acid-free paper by
Halstan & Co. Ltd., Amersham, Bucks.

Text by Laurence Housman reprinted by permission of The Random House
Group (UK).

Attack by Siegfried Sassoon reprinted by permission of George Sassoon for the
United Kingdom and Commonwealth. For the United States of America
copyright 1918 by E.P. Dutton, renewed © 1946 by Siegfried Sassoon, from
Collected Poems of Siegfried Sassoon, and used by permission of Viking Penguin,
a division of Penguin Putnam Inc.

Cover photograph: still from the film *The Battle of the Somme* (1916) by permission
of The Trustees of the Imperial War Museum, London. Crown copyright,
reproduced by permission of the Controller of Her Majesty's Stationery Office.

CONTENTS

ORCHESTRATION

2 flutes
oboe
2 clarinets
bassoon
2 horns
2 trumpets

2 percussion

glockenspiel	bell (G)
snare drum	triangle
suspended cymbal	gong
clashed cymbals	whip
bass drum	

timpani (3 pedal timpani)
harp
strings

Lux Perpetua was commissioned by the Hinsdale Township High School District 86, Music Director, Gary L. Wilhelm. It was first performed by the combined choirs and orchestra of Hinsdale High Schools, Chicago, on 23 March 1999, conducted by the composer.

Full score and parts are available from the publisher's Hire Library.

Duration: *c.* 30 minutes

The initial stimulus to write *Lux Perpetua* was a commission for a choral piece on the theme of 'Peace and Unity'. By coincidence, the time when I was considering the structure of the work and texts that might be included coincided with the eightieth anniversary of the November 1918 armistice and I spent a few days amongst the battlefields and endless cemeteries of the Great War in Flanders. There can surely be no more moving symbol of the destruction and futility of human conflict. Two months later, as I was nearing completion of the composition, my youngest child, Florence, was born. A new-born child - the innocence and hope of the world. And then, on the very night of the first performance of the work in March 1999, allied forces began saturation bombing of Kosovo in a conflict that was to prove yet again that in war there are rarely winners, but always many who suffer.

Jonathan Willcocks

Requiem aeternam dona eis, Domine, et lux perpetua luceat eis.　　　　　From the Requiem Mass

The day will come when I will make for you a covenant with the beasts of the fields,　　　From the Oxford Book of Prayer
the birds of the air, and the insects of the ground; and I will remove the bow, the sword,
and war from the earth, and I will give you a life of peace.

Kyrie eleison, Christe eleison, Kyrie eleison

An army marches into war.　　　　　Jonathan Willcocks
From the darkness a conflict beckons, menacing every soul.
Officers drive men forward, the ranks respond with resolute stride and innocent pride,
the battle is joined.

As wave on wave of raw humanity, fresh to the blade,
knowing little of the menace of the whetstone.
Life's flickering spark snuffed dark,
so deadly a hand reaping the human harvest drawn to the sickle.

An army marches into war.
They hurl themselves to the perils that others have made.
Dear Lord, in your mercy, must it be so?
Sweet heav'n show us the way we may go.

Be silent and I will speak, listen to me, be silent and I will teach you wisdom.　　　　　Job 33

Kyrie eleison, Christe eleison, Kyrie eleison

Light looked down and beheld Darkness　　So came Light and shone;　　　　　Laurence Housman (1865-1959)
Thither will I go, said Light.　　　　So came Peace and gave rest;
Peace looked down and beheld War,　　So came Love and brought Life.
Thither will I go, said Peace.　　　　And the Word was made Flesh and dwelt
Love looked down and beheld Hatred,　　among us.
Thither will I go, said Love.

Let us be united; let us speak in harmony; common be our prayer; perfect be our unity.　　　　　from Hindu scriptures

Kyrie eleison, Christe eleison, Kyrie eleison

At dawn the ridge emerges massed and dun　　　　　Siegfried Sassoon (1886-1967)
In the wild purple of the glow'ring sun,
Smouldering through spouts of drifting smoke that shroud
The menacing scarred slope; and, one by one,
Tanks creep and topple forward to the wire.
The barrage roars and lifts. Then, clumsily bowed
With bombs and guns and shovels and battle-gear,
Men jostle and climb to meet the bristling fire.
Lines of grey, muttering faces, masked with fear,
They leave their trenches, going over the top,
While time ticks blank and busy on their wrists,
And hope, with furtive eyes and grappling fists,
Flounders in mud. O Jesus, make it stop.

Show us thy mercy, O Lord; and grant us thy salvation.　　　　　from Psalm 85

Kyrie eleison, Christe eleison, Kyrie eleison

Lord, make me an instrument of Thy peace;　　Where there is doubt, faith;　　　　　St. Francis of Assisi (1182-1226)
Where there is hatred, let me sow love;　　Where there is despair, hope;
Where there is injury, pardon;　　　　Where there is darkness, light;
Where there is discord, union;　　　　Where there is sadness, joy.

Et lux perpetua luceat eis.

May we all be in peace, peace, and only peace; and may that peace come unto each of us　　　　　Indian - The Vedas

Gather us in, Thou love that fillest all;　　　　　G. D. Matheson (1842-1906)
Gather our rival faiths within thy fold.
Rend each man's temple-veil and bid it fall,
That we may know that Thou hast been of old;

Gather us in: we worship only Thee;　　　　Each sees one colour of thy rainbow-light,
In varied names we stretch a common hand;　　Each looks upon one tint and calls it heaven;
In diverse forms a common soul we see;　　Thou art the fullness of our partial sight;
In many ships we seek one spirit-land;　　We are not perfect till we find the seven;

As we are together, praying for Peace.　　　　　Buddhist Litany for peace

Requiescant in pace. Amen.

Commissioned by Hinsdale Township High School District 86
Music Director Gary L. Wilhelm

LUX PERPETUA
1

JONATHAN WILLCOCKS

Printed in Great Britain

OXFORD UNIVERSITY PRESS, MUSIC DEPARTMENT, GREAT CLARENDON STREET, OXFORD OX2 6DP

A

et lux per-pe - tu -
et lux_____ per -
_____ do-mi - - - ne.
- ne,_____

(bell)

-a, lu - ce - at_____ e - - is._____
-pe - tu - a,_____ lu-ce-at_____ e - is._____

(bell)

4

ground; and I will re-move the bow, the sword, and war from the earth, and I will

give you, and I will give you a life of peace,____ a life of

and I will give you, will give a life__ of peace,____

C

peace,____ of peace.____

(bell)

6

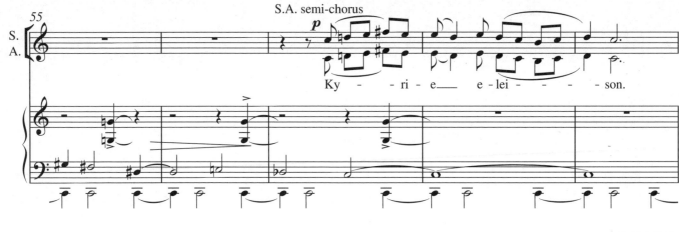

S.A. semi-chorus

S.
A.

Ky - ri - e___ e - lei - - son.

Chri - - - - ste e - lei - son.___

(bell)

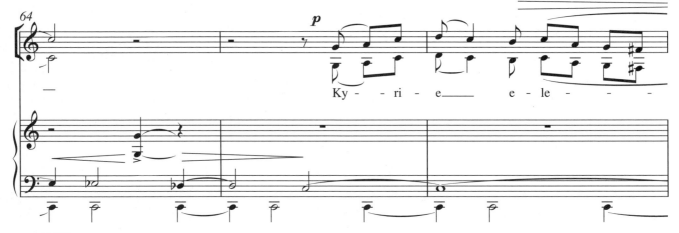

Ky - ri - e___ e - le - -

- son.

dying away

2

D

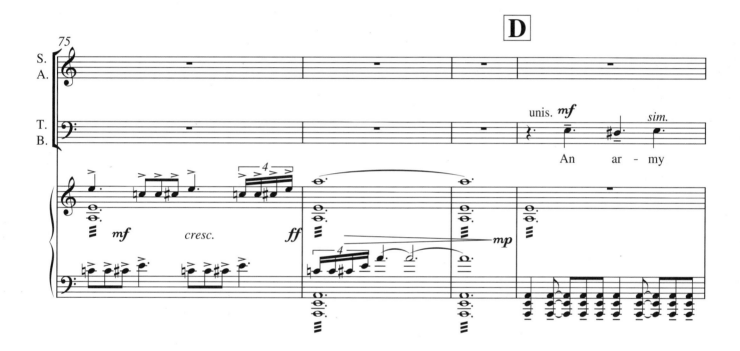

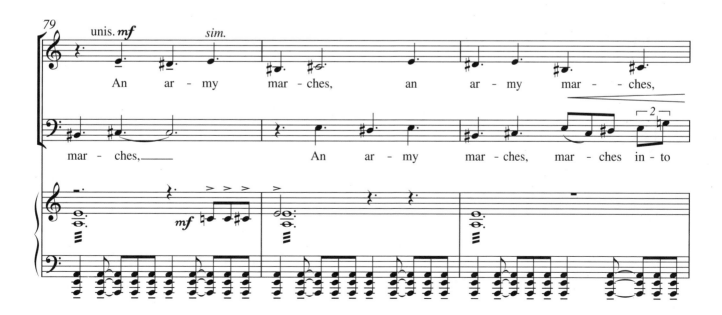

marches into war.

war.

An

An ar - my marches, marches into war.

ar - my marches, marches into war.

From the

E

From the dark - ness a con - flict bec - kons,

dark - ness a con - flict bec - kons, me - na - cing ev-ery soul. From the

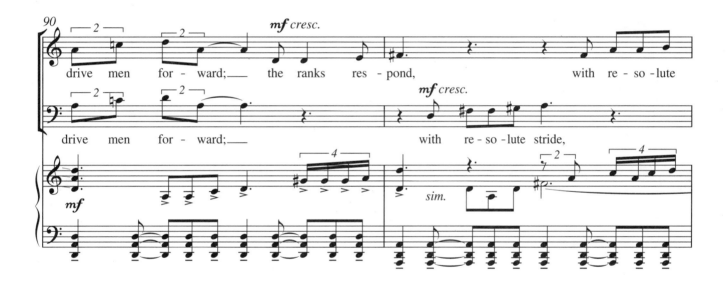

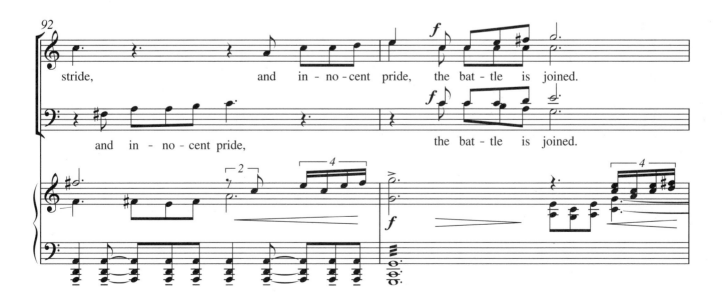

the bat - tle is joined. As wave on

wave of raw hu - - ma - ni - ty,_____ fresh to the

blade, know - ing lit - tle of the me - - - - nace of _ the

whet - stone.   Life's flick - er - ing   spark_____ snuffed   dark,_____ so

dead - ly   a   hand_____ rea - ping,   rea - ping,   rea - ping____

_____ the hu - man har - vest drawn to the sic-kle.

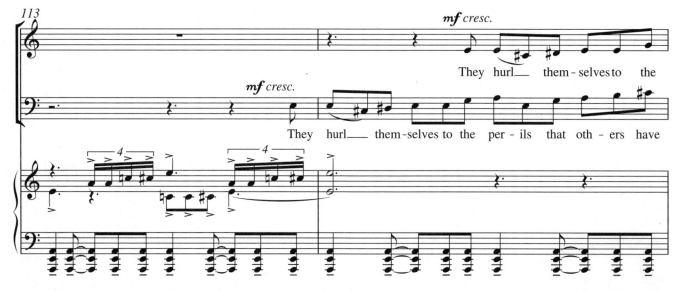

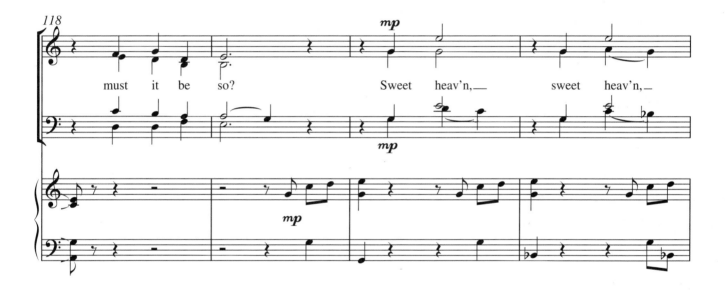

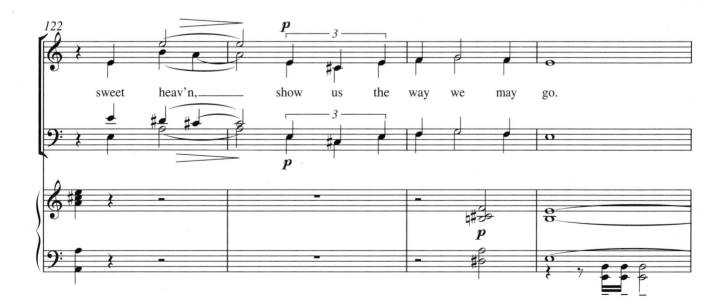

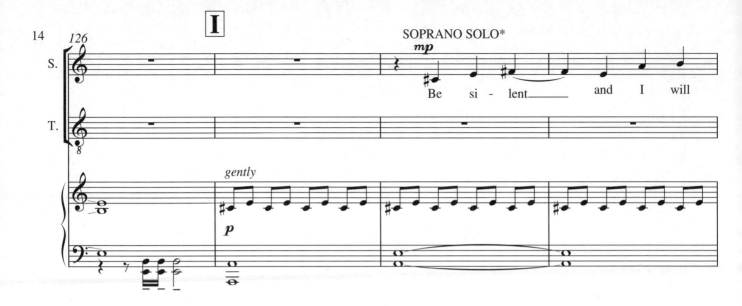

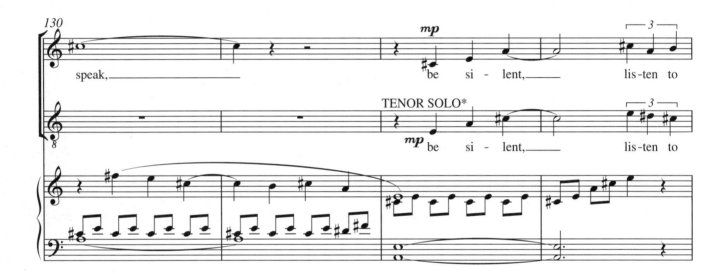

(or semichorus). Solo voices should be, if possible, from within the choir.

3

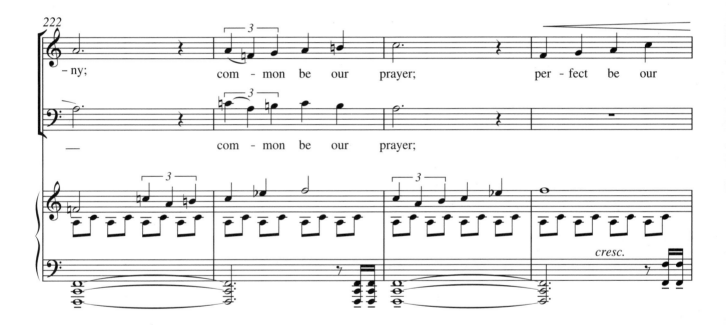

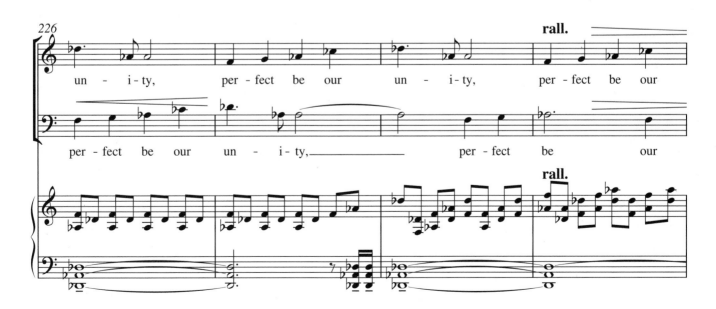

4

At dawn the ridge e - - mer - ges massed and

dun in the wild pur - ple of the glow - 'ring sun,

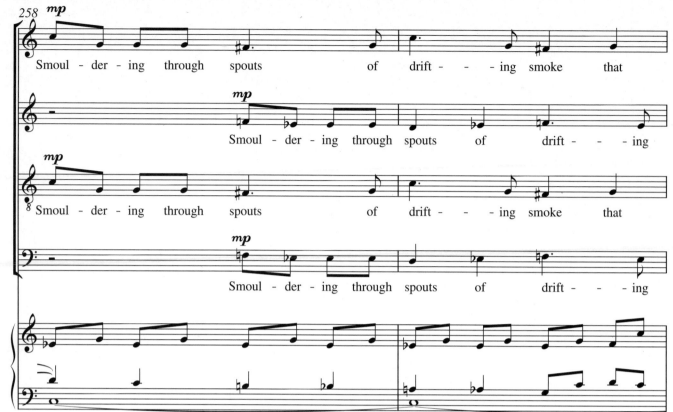

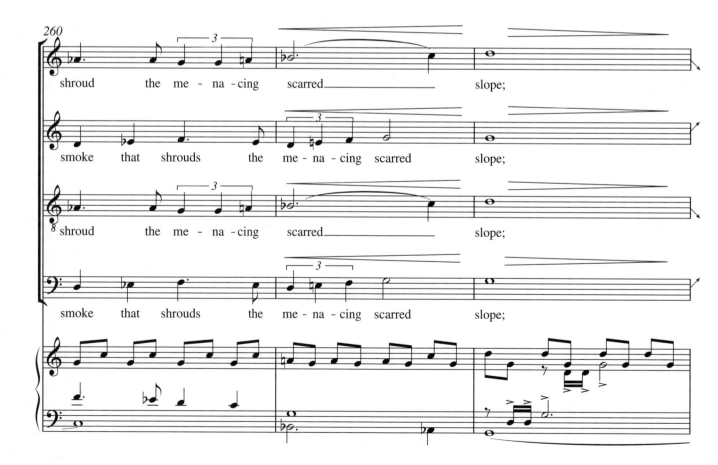

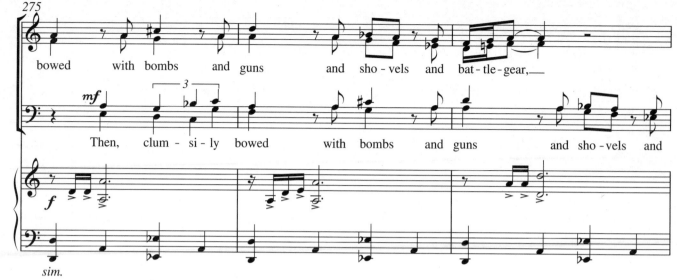

275

bowed   with   bombs   and   guns   and   sho - vels   and   bat - tle - gear,___

Then,   clum - si - ly   bowed   with   bombs   and   guns   and   sho - vels   and

278   **poco a poco accel.**

men   jos - tle   and   climb   to   meet   the   brist - ling

bat - tle - gear,___

poco a poco accel.

281

fire.   Lines   of   grey,   mut - tering   fa - ces,   masked   with   fear,

30

5

For Florence, newly born, the innocence and hope of the world

Lord, make me an in - stru - ment of Thy peace; where there is ha - tred, let me sow love; where there is in - - ju - ry, par - don; where_____ there is dis - cord, may there be

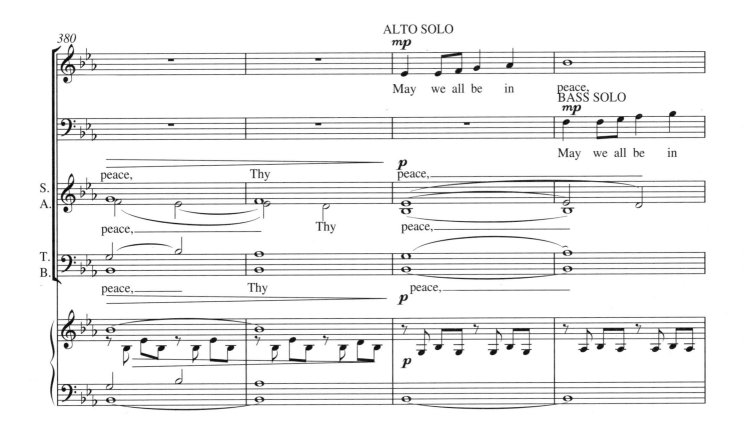

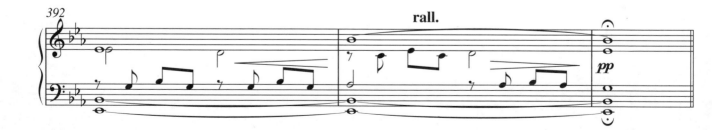

6

SOLI

44

V

SOLI

peace.

Ga - ther us in,   ga -ther us in.

Ga - ther us in,   ga -ther us, ga - ther us in.

Ga - ther us in,   ga - ther us ga - - ther us in.

Gather us in   ga-ther us in.

(bell)

Each sees one co-lour of thy rain - bow - light,   each looks up-on   one tint and calls   it

heaven;   Thou art the full - ness   of   our   par - - tial   sight;

we are not per - fect till we find the seven;

S.

Ga - ther us in.

A.

Ga - ther us in, ga - ther us, ga - - - ther us in,

T.

Ga - ther us in, ga - ther us in.

B.

Ga - ther us in, ga - ther us in,

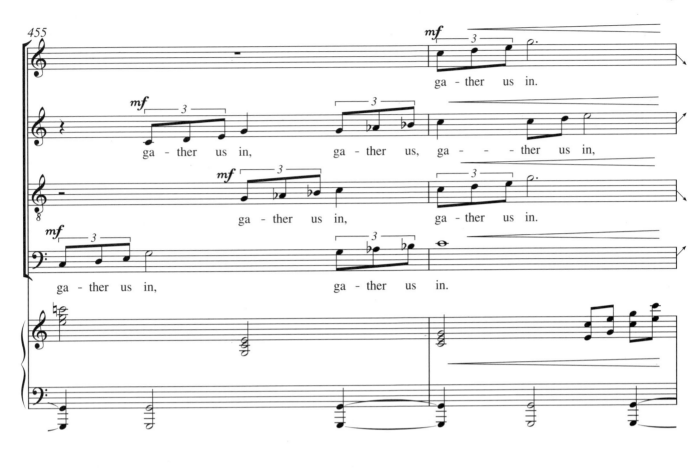

W